Animals on the Farm

Ducks

Linda Aspen-Baxter

www.av2books.com

D0503306

Go to **www.av2books.com,** and enter this book's unique code.

BOOK CODE

H 5 4 5 4 8 5

AV² by Weigl brings you media enhanced books that support active learning.

AV² provides enriched content that supplements and complements this book. Weigl's AV² books strive to create inspired learning and engage young minds in a total learning experience.

Your AV² Media Enhanced books come alive with...

Audio
Listen to sections of the book read aloud.

Video
Watch informative video clips.

Embedded Weblinks
Gain additional information for research.

Try This!
Complete activities and hands-on experiments.

Key Words
Study vocabulary, and complete a matching word activity.

Quizzes
Test your knowledge.

Slide Show
View images and captions, and prepare a presentation.

... and much, much more!

Published by AV² by Weigl
350 5th Avenue, 59th Floor New York, NY 10118
Website: www.av2books.com   www.weigl.com

Aspen-Baxter, Linda.
 Ducks / Linda Aspen-Baxter.
   p. cm. -- (Animals on the farm)
 ISBN 978-1-61690-926-0 (hardcover : alk. paper) -- ISBN 978-1-61690-572-9 (online)
 1. Ducks--Juvenile literature. I. Title.
 SF505.3.K57 2012
 636.5'97--dc23
                    2011023419

Printed in the United States of America in North Mankato, Minnesota
1 2 3 4 5 6 7 8 9 0 15 14 13 12 11

062011
WEP030611

Senior Editor: Heather Kissock   Art Director: Terry Paulhus

Weigl acknowledges Getty Images as the primary image supplier for this title.

Animals on the Farm

Ducks

CONTENTS

I am a small farm animal. Farmers keep me for eggs and feathers.

5

I am a bird. I have feathers on my body and wings.

7

I walk on two legs on land.
My webbed feet help me swim.
Oil on my feathers keeps me dry.

My eyes are on the sides of my head. I do not have to turn my head to see all around. This helps me find food.

I use my bill
to hunt for food.
I like to eat seeds,
grass, worms,
and bugs.

How do I talk to other ducks?
I quack and whistle.

15

I like to be with other ducks.
We can be very noisy!

17

My babies hatch from eggs.

My ducklings eat on their own.

My babies want to be like the first living thing they see. It should be me. It can also be a person or an animal!

21

DUCK FACTS

This page provides more detail about the interesting facts found in the book. Simply look at the corresponding page number to match the fact.

Pages 4-5

A duck is a small farm animal. Farmers keep ducks for eggs and feathers. Farmers also raise ducks for meat. People use duck feathers to stuff pillows, coats, and quilts. Other ducks are kept as pets or for show. Most farm ducks are Pekin. They have white or cream feathers and an orange bill. Pekin ducks cannot fly.

Pages 6–7

Ducks are birds. They have feathers on their body and wings. Birds are the only animals to have this feature. Birds share other features as well. All birds are vertebrates. They also have a bill for a mouth and produce young by laying eggs. Most people associate birds with flight. While most birds do fly, there are several types that cannot.

Pages 8–9

Ducks walk on two legs on land. Their webbed feet help them swim. Oil on their feathers keeps them dry. Ducks have a gland near their tail that makes a special oil. They use their bills to spread this oil on their feathers to make them waterproof. Ducks can stay in water for a long time because their feet do not get cold. Their feet have no nerves or blood vessels.

Pages 10–11

A duck's eyes are on the sides of its head. It does not have to turn its head to see all around. This helps the duck find food. It also helps ducks watch for predators, such as raccoons, owls, hawks, foxes, and coyotes. Most domestic ducks cannot fly away from predators, so it is important for farmers to provide them with a safe shelter.